TREVOR ANDERSON

Click Smart, Stay Safe

The Essential Guide to Digital Safety and Awareness

Copyright © 2024 by Trevor Anderson

All rights reserved. No part of this publication may be reproduced, stored or transmitted in any form or by any means, electronic, mechanical, photocopying, recording, scanning, or otherwise without written permission from the publisher. It is illegal to copy this book, post it to a website, or distribute it by any other means without permission.

First edition

This book was professionally typeset on Reedsy. Find out more at reedsy.com

Contents

Introduction	1
1 Welcome to the Digital World	3
2 Privacy Matters	7
3 Spotting Scams and Online Threats	11
4 Guarding Your Devices and Accounts	16
5 Navigating Social Media Safely	21
6 Smart Habits for Digital Wellness	26
7 Recognizing and Avoiding Online Scams	31
8 Protecting Your Digital Identity	36
9 Building a Responsible and Positive Digital Reputation	41
10 Bringing It All Together: Your Path to a Safer Digital Life	46
Glossary	51
Citation	54
Disclaimer	56

Introduction

The digital world is vast, exciting, and full of possibilities. From staying in touch with family and friends to learning new skills, sharing ideas, and exploring interests, the internet has transformed how we connect, work, and play. But along with these amazing opportunities come some risks and navigating them wisely has never been more important.

In today's world, our devices connect us to almost everything, and our online actions can impact our personal and professional lives in ways we might not expect. Just as we learn safety rules for the real world—like looking both ways before crossing the street or locking the door when we leave the house—it's essential to understand the "rules of the road" for digital safety. Without a guide, it's easy to overlook these risks, but a little knowledge can make a big difference. That's where this book comes in.

Who Is This Book For?

Click Smart, Stay Safe is for anyone—teens, parents, students, professionals—who want to gain the skills and knowledge needed to stay safe and make wise choices in a digital world. Whether you're a seasoned internet user or just starting to explore online spaces, this guide is designed to be your essential companion, helping you feel confident and informed as you navigate your digital life.

What You'll Learn

In this book, you'll explore topics that help you protect your privacy, keep your personal information secure, and understand the common digital threats that can arise. Each chapter covers a specific area of digital safety, including recognizing online threats, using social media responsibly, preventing cyberbullying, and protecting your online reputation. You'll also learn practical, real-world strategies for keeping your devices secure and managing your digital identity, with interactive activities and takeaways that bring each topic to life.

Why Digital Safety Matters

In the fast-evolving online landscape, understanding how to protect yourself isn't just a good idea—it's essential. With online scams, misinformation, and privacy breaches on the rise, knowing the basics of digital safety helps you make empowered choices, avoid risks, and become a thoughtful, responsible digital citizen. A secure online experience allows you to focus on what matters most: connecting, creating, and learning in ways that benefit you and those around you.

How to Use This Book

Each chapter in Click Smart, Stay Safe builds on the last, providing you with essential tools and tips to develop a comprehensive understanding of digital safety. Every chapter concludes with key takeaways and a hands-on activity to help you apply what you've learned. By the end, you'll have a solid foundation for navigating the digital world with confidence.

So, get ready to dive in! Your journey to a safer, smarter digital experience starts here. Let's explore how to click smart and stay safe as you become empowered to make the most of your online world.

1

Welcome to the Digital World

In today's digital age, being online has become as common as having electricity or running water. Whether we're checking social media, shopping, streaming, or working, our connection to the digital world is nearly constant. But with all the convenience and information the internet offers, it also brings unique challenges, like protecting privacy, recognizing scams, and building a positive online reputation. This chapter will introduce you to digital literacy, and the core concepts of navigating the online world wisely and safely.

What is Digital Literacy?

Digital literacy is the ability to navigate, understand, and engage with digital information and technology responsibly. It's not just about knowing how to use a smartphone or log into a social media account. Digital literacy includes understanding the importance of privacy, evaluating the accuracy of online information, and interacting with others respectfully.

Think of it as learning to read and write in the digital world. Just as literacy in reading helps us understand books, literacy in the digital world helps us make sense of everything we encounter online. A solid foundation in digital literacy can make the internet a safer, more empowering place.

The History of the Internet and the Rise of Digital Safety Concerns

The internet began as a project in the 1960s, created by a few researchers wanting to connect computers for faster information sharing. By the 1990s, it had grown into a worldwide network accessible to the public. With this growth came vast opportunities but also new risks. As more people shared personal information online, scammers, hackers, and advertisers quickly learned to exploit this data.

Initially, safety issues were relatively simple, like avoiding email scams or keeping personal information private on websites. However, as technology advanced, online dangers became more sophisticated, requiring users to develop critical skills for protection. Today, digital safety is a complex and essential part of daily life.

Understanding Your Digital Footprint

Every action we take online—whether liking a post, shopping or sending an email—creates a trail known as a "digital footprint." This footprint can be tracked and stored, sometimes permanently. Imagine you're walking through fresh snow; every step leaves an impression. Similarly, each online activity leaves an impression, visible to others and, in some cases, accessible to websites or even search engines.

There are two types of digital footprints: **active** and **passive**. An active footprint is something we knowingly create, like a social media post or a comment. A passive footprint, however, is created without our direct input—such as when a website tracks our visits, or an app logs our location.

Being aware of your digital footprint helps you make informed choices about what to share online. It's essential to remember that once something is online, it may be very difficult to remove entirely.

WELCOME TO THE DIGITAL WORLD

Why Digital Literacy and Safety Matter

Just like learning to cross a busy street, understanding the digital world's complexities helps protect us. Here are a few key reasons why digital literacy and safety are important for everyone:

- **Privacy Protection**: With the amount of personal information shared online, it's crucial to understand how to control and protect that data.
- **Reputation Management**: Digital footprints affect our reputations, sometimes impacting opportunities or relationships.
- **Scam Prevention**: Being able to recognize and avoid scams saves us from possible financial loss and identity theft.
- **Effective Communication**: Knowing how to communicate respectfully and responsibly online promotes positive relationships and reduces the risk of misunderstandings.

Developing digital literacy allows us to make the most of what the internet offers while minimizing risks. Each chapter in this book will build on this foundation, giving you tools to navigate online spaces with confidence.

Key Takeaways

- **Digital literacy** is the skill set that helps us safely navigate the online world.
- Our **digital footprint** is the record of everything we do online, and it can be challenging to erase.
- Understanding and practicing digital literacy helps us protect privacy, manage our reputations, avoid scams, and communicate effectively.

Interactive Activity: Digital Footprint Reflection

Take a moment to think about your online activities over the past week. Make a quick list of your interactions, such as:

- Posts or comments made on social media
- Online shopping activities
- Websites visited for information or entertainment
- Messages or emails sent

Once you've listed these, ask yourself:

- Would I be comfortable if a family member, friend, or colleague saw each of these interactions?
- Is there anything I would want to keep private, or perhaps delete if possible?

By reflecting on these questions, you're taking a first step toward managing your digital footprint. This awareness will be a valuable tool as we explore other aspects of online safety in the following chapters.

2

Privacy Matters

Online privacy has become one of the most pressing concerns of the digital age. Every time we sign up for a new app, click "accept" on a website or even just browse the internet, we're potentially sharing information about ourselves. From names and email addresses to browsing habits and location data, our personal information is valuable—not just to us, but to companies, advertisers, and sometimes even hackers. This chapter dives into the basics of protecting your privacy online and offers simple yet effective tips to keep your data secure.

Understanding Personal Data and Why It's Valuable

Every click, post, or app download generates data that can be collected, shared, and sometimes sold. But what exactly is personal data? It's any information that can identify you as an individual, such as:

- **Contact Information**: Your name, email address, and phone number.
- **Financial Information**: Credit card numbers or payment details.
- **Location Data**: Where you live, or even your real-time location

when using apps.
- **Behavioral Information**: The types of websites you visit, how often, and what you search for online.

Companies collect this data because it helps them improve products, target ads, and sometimes sell insights to third parties. While some data collection can be beneficial (such as improving the user experience), knowing how to control and protect this information is key to maintaining privacy.

Creating Strong Passwords and Managing Them Safely

Passwords are your first line of defense against unauthorized access to your online accounts. However, not all passwords are created equal. Passwords like "123456" or "password" are easy to remember, but they're also incredibly easy for hackers to guess.

Here's how to create strong passwords:

- **Use a Mix of Characters**: Combine upper and lowercase letters, numbers, and symbols.
- **Make it Long**: Aim for at least 12 characters.
- **Avoid Personal Info**: Don't include easily guessed information, like your name or birthdate.
- **Use a Passphrase**: Choose a random phrase (e.g., "BlueSky&PurpleSunset") that's easy to remember but hard to guess.

To keep track of complex passwords, consider using a **password manager**. These tools securely store and manage your passwords, so you only need to remember one master password. Some popular options include LastPass, 1Password, and Bitwarden.

Data Collection and Permissions: What Apps and Websites Are

PRIVACY MATTERS

Really Accessing

Most apps and websites ask for certain permissions—access to your location, camera, microphone, and contacts, for example. But not every app actually needs this data to function properly. Reviewing and controlling app permissions helps protect your privacy and limit data collection.

Here's how to manage permissions on your devices:

- **Check App Settings**: On both iOS and Android, you can go to your settings and review permissions for each app. Disable permissions that feel unnecessary.
- **Beware of Default Settings**: Many apps default to maximum permissions. Always review settings after downloading a new app.
- **Location Sharing**: Unless it's essential, keep location tracking to "while using the app" or turn it off entirely.

By managing permissions, you limit what apps and websites can access and reduce the risk of oversharing data without knowing it.

Key Takeaways

- Personal data, including contact, financial, and location information, is valuable to companies and can be exploited by hackers.
- Strong, unique passwords are essential for keeping your accounts secure. Consider using a password manager to help.
- Limiting app and website permissions helps control the data you share, reducing unnecessary privacy risks.

Interactive Activity: Privacy Settings Checkup

For this activity, let's take a hands-on approach to improving your online privacy by reviewing your account settings:

1. **Pick Two Accounts**: Choose two frequently used accounts (such as social media or email) and log in.
2. **Check Privacy Settings**: Go to the account settings and review the privacy options available. Look for options to limit who can see your profile information, posts, or other personal details.
3. **Adjust Permissions**: Turn off any unnecessary permissions for each account, like location tracking or app access to your contacts.
4. **Set Strong Passwords**: If you're not using strong passwords on these accounts, take a moment to change them to something secure, using the password guidelines from this chapter.

This simple checkup can go a long way in helping protect your personal data and strengthen your online privacy. Repeat this activity periodically as a routine check on your digital safety.

3

Spotting Scams and Online Threats

As we spend more time online, scammers, hackers, and fraudsters are constantly coming up with new tricks to steal our information, money, or both. While some scams are easy to recognize, others can be very convincing. This chapter will help you understand common online threats, recognize the red flags of scams, and take steps to keep your personal information safe from prying eyes.

Common Types of Online Scams

Scammers often prey on emotions like excitement, fear, or urgency to get people to act without thinking. Here are some of the most common types of scams you may encounter online:

1. **Phishing Emails and Messages**: Phishing scams are fake emails, texts, or social media messages that appear to be from a legitimate source (like a bank or government agency). They usually ask for sensitive information, such as login credentials or credit card details.
2. **Fake Tech Support**: In these scams, the fraudster pretends to be a tech support representative, warning you about a supposed "virus"

on your device. They might ask you to pay for a solution or allow remote access to your computer, which can lead to a data breach.
3. **Online Shopping Scams**: Some fake websites or social media ads offer incredible deals on popular items. But once you pay, the item either doesn't arrive or isn't as advertised. Checking for verified sellers and reading reviews can help you avoid this trap.
4. **Investment Scams**: These scams often promote "too good to be true" investment opportunities, promising big returns with little risk. They may involve fake cryptocurrency schemes or social media influencers claiming to make huge profits. Always be wary of unsolicited investment offers.
5. **Fake Contests or "Congratulations" Messages**: These are pop-ups or emails telling you that you've "won" a prize but must enter personal details or pay a fee to claim it. Legitimate contests don't ask for payments to claim prizes.

Knowing these common scams can help you spot threats more easily and avoid falling victim to them.

Red Flags to Watch For

Scams can be sneaky, but they often share some common warning signs. Here are a few red flags to help you identify potential scams:

- **Urgency**: Messages that create a sense of urgency, like "Act now!" or "You only have 24 hours to respond!" Scammers often use urgency to get you to act before you have time to think.
- **Poor Grammar and Spelling**: Many scam emails and messages contain grammar mistakes or awkward wording. If a message from a reputable source has multiple errors, it's a warning sign.
- **Suspicious Links**: Scam messages often contain links that lead to fake websites. Hover over the link (without clicking!) to see the

SPOTTING SCAMS AND ONLINE THREATS

actual web address and check if it looks legitimate.
- **Requests for Personal or Financial Information**: No trustworthy organization will ask for sensitive information (like Social Security numbers or passwords) over email or text.
- **Too-Good-to-Be-True Offers**: If something sounds too good to be true—like a free vacation or easy money from a stranger—it probably is.

Keeping these red flags in mind will help you make better judgments about messages or offers that come your way.

How to Protect Yourself from Scams

Being aware of scams is essential, but taking steps to protect yourself is even better. Here are some strategies for staying safe:

- **Don't Click on Suspicious Links**: If you receive an email or message with a link that seems off, don't click it. Go directly to the official website to log in or verify any claims.
- **Use Two-Factor Authentication (2FA)**: Enabling 2FA adds an extra layer of security to your accounts. Even if a scammer manages to steal your password, they'll need a second form of verification (like a code sent to your phone) to log in.
- **Verify Before You Trust**: If someone contacts you claiming to be from a company or organization, don't give out information right away. Call the official customer service line or check the official website to verify.
- **Keep Software Updated**: Updating your apps and devices regularly helps protect you from security vulnerabilities that scammers might exploit.
- **Report Scams**: If you come across a scam, report it to the platform where it appeared (like social media or email) or to your local

consumer protection agency. Reporting scams helps keep others safe as well.

Key Takeaways

- Scammers often use emotions like excitement, fear, or urgency to trick people into giving up personal information.
- Watch for red flags, including poor grammar, suspicious links, and unsolicited requests for personal or financial information.
- Take proactive steps like enabling two-factor authentication and verifying messages to protect yourself from online threats.

Interactive Activity: Real or Scam?

Now that you know more about scams, let's practice identifying them. Here's a scenario exercise:

1. **Scenario A:** You receive an email from what appears to be your bank, saying there's been suspicious activity on your account and asking you to confirm your password by clicking a link.
2. **Scenario B:** A pop-up ad claims you've won a new iPhone and need to enter your personal information to claim it.
3. **Scenario C:** A social media friend sends a direct message asking for your help in transferring some money, promising to pay you a percentage.

For each scenario, decide if it's a potential scam, and then list the red flags that led you to your decision.

By the end of this chapter, you'll have a solid understanding of

SPOTTING SCAMS AND ONLINE THREATS

common online threats and the tools to recognize and respond to them. Recognizing scams is the first step toward staying safe in the digital world.

4

Guarding Your Devices and Accounts

In today's interconnected world, our devices and online accounts hold a treasure trove of personal information—photos, messages, financial data, and more. Keeping these secure isn't just about protecting your privacy; it's about preserving your identity and your online reputation. In this chapter, we'll explore key steps to protect your devices and accounts from unauthorized access, hacks, and data loss.

Securing Your Devices

Your devices—whether a smartphone, laptop, or tablet—are the entry points to your online life. Keeping them secure is the first line of defense against potential threats. Here are some essential strategies:

1. **Enable Device Locks**: Use a PIN, password, or biometric lock (like fingerprint or facial recognition) on all your devices. This simple step prevents others from easily accessing your data if your device is lost or stolen.
2. **Install Security Software**: Anti-virus and anti-malware programs are critical for detecting and blocking harmful software.

GUARDING YOUR DEVICES AND ACCOUNTS

Even mobile devices benefit from security apps that guard against malicious downloads or suspicious activity.
3. **Regularly Update Software**: Software updates often include important security patches that fix vulnerabilities. By keeping your operating system and apps up to date, you're better protected from threats.
4. **Be Careful with Public Wi-Fi**: Public networks are often unsecured, making it easier for hackers to intercept data. If you must use public Wi-Fi, avoid accessing sensitive accounts, and consider using a **Virtual Private Network (VPN)** to protect your data.
5. **Turn Off Bluetooth and Location Services When Not in Use**: Bluetooth and location tracking can expose your device to risks when left on. Disabling these features when they aren't needed can reduce your vulnerability.

By following these steps, you make it much harder for unauthorized users to access your devices and the data they hold.

Protecting Your Online Accounts

Online accounts—social media, email, bank accounts—are valuable and often targeted by hackers. Protecting them requires smart practices, from creating strong passwords to recognizing suspicious login attempts. Here's how to secure your accounts:

1. **Create Unique Passwords**: Each account should have its own password. If a hacker gains access to one account, they won't be able to use the same password to access others.
2. **Enable Two-Factor Authentication (2FA)**: Adding a second layer of security requires you to confirm your identity with a code sent to your phone or email, making it harder for hackers to get into

your accounts.

3. **Be Wary of Unfamiliar Logins and Notifications**: Most services alert you if there's an unusual login attempt on your account. Take these seriously and check your account settings to see if anything was compromised.
4. **Limit Third-Party App Access**: Apps and websites sometimes ask for permission to access your main accounts, like social media or Google. Only grant permissions to trusted apps, and periodically review and remove permissions from apps you no longer use.
5. **Use Account Recovery Options**: Set up account recovery options, such as backup email addresses or security questions. This way, if you lose access to your account, you have an alternative way to regain control.

Recognizing and Avoiding Phishing Attempts

Phishing is one of the most common methods hackers use to trick people into giving up account credentials. Phishing messages look like they're from trusted sources but often lead to fake websites designed to steal your information. Here are some tips to avoid falling victim to phishing:

- **Examine the Email or Message Closely**: Check the sender's address carefully. Phishing emails often come from slightly altered addresses (e.g., support@yourbankk.com instead of support@your bank.com).
- **Don't Click on Links from Unknown Sources**: If you're unsure about a link, hover over it to view the URL, or go directly to the official website instead.
- **Look for Generic Greetings and Urgent Language**: Phishing

emails may start with "Dear User" instead of your name and often try to create a sense of urgency, like "Your account will be locked if you don't respond within 24 hours."
- **Use Browser Extensions for Phishing Protection**: Some web browsers and security software offer tools that warn you when you're about to enter a suspicious or fake site.

Key Takeaways

- Keeping devices secure through strong locks, updates, and cautious use of public Wi-Fi is essential for protecting your information.
- Online accounts are best protected by unique passwords, two-factor authentication, and being cautious about third-party app access.
- Phishing attempts are common threats; avoid them by examining emails carefully, not clicking on suspicious links, and using browser extensions for additional protection.

Interactive Activity: Securing Your Accounts

This activity will guide you through a practical exercise in strengthening your account security. Follow these steps:

1. **Select Three Accounts**: Pick three accounts that you use often (such as social media, email, or a bank account).
2. **Update Passwords and Enable 2FA**: Check that each account has a strong, unique password. If you haven't done so already, enable two-factor authentication on these accounts.
3. **Review Connected Apps and Permissions**: Log into each account and review any third-party apps that have access. Revoke permissions for apps you no longer use or don't fully trust.

4. **Practice Phishing Awareness**: Open your email inbox and scan for any messages that seem suspicious. Look at the sender address and any links to see if you can identify common phishing tactics.

By securing your accounts with these steps, you're building a foundation of digital safety that will help protect your information from unwanted access.

5

Navigating Social Media Safely

Social media connects us with friends, family, and communities worldwide, allowing us to share moments, ideas, and news. However, it also brings unique risks, from oversharing personal details to encountering harmful content or falling victim to scams. This chapter offers strategies to help you navigate social media safely, manage your online presence, and set boundaries that protect both your privacy and well-being.

Understanding Social Media Privacy Settings

Privacy settings are essential tools that control who can see your posts, photos, and personal information on social media platforms. Each platform offers different options, so it's essential to familiarize yourself with them and adjust the settings to suit your comfort level.

1. **Audience Selection**: Most platforms allow you to choose your audience—public, friends only, or custom groups. Regularly review your posts' audience to make sure you're sharing with the people you intend to reach.
2. **Profile Visibility**: Some platforms allow you to limit what others

see when they view your profile. For example, you may want to hide your phone number, email, or location from people you aren't directly connected to.
3. **Activity and Location Sharing**: Many social media platforms let you tag locations or share live locations in posts. While this can be fun, it's best to turn off location tagging by default and only enable it for specific, trusted posts.
4. **Limit Data Sharing with Third-Party Apps**: Sometimes, we use third-party apps that connect to our social media profiles. Review which apps have access to your account data, and revoke permissions for any that you don't recognize or use.

Taking a few minutes to adjust these settings can go a long way in helping you keep your information private and under control.

Avoiding Oversharing: What Not to Post

Oversharing can inadvertently put you at risk by revealing sensitive details that others could exploit. Here are some examples of things to avoid posting:

- **Personal Identifiers**: Avoid sharing your home address, phone number, or even your full birth date, as these details can be used for identity theft.
- **Travel Plans**: While it's exciting to share about an upcoming trip, consider waiting until after you return to post travel details. Posting travel plans can alert people to the fact that your home may be empty.
- **Work-Related Information**: Avoid sharing sensitive work details or information about colleagues or projects, as this can sometimes breach company policies or lead to security risks.
- **Photos with Sensitive Information**: Be cautious about photos

that might unintentionally reveal personal information, like pictures of tickets, bills, or even family photos that show your address in the background.

Being mindful of what you post can help protect your privacy and reduce potential risks.

Identifying and Dealing with Harmful Content

Social media can expose users to a range of harmful content, from online harassment to misinformation. Here's how to recognize and manage these situations:

1. **Recognizing Fake News and Misinformation**: Some posts may spread false information, either intentionally or unintentionally. Before sharing, verify the source of any news by checking for reliable, reputable sources. Platforms often flag disputed content, but it's always good to fact-check on your own.
2. **Blocking and Reporting**: Most platforms allow you to block or report users who engage in harassment or post offensive content. Don't hesitate to use these tools if you feel uncomfortable or threatened.
3. **Controlling Comments and Messages**: Some platforms let you limit who can comment on your posts or send you messages. Adjust these settings to prevent unwanted contact, especially from people you don't know.
4. **Taking Breaks When Needed**: Social media can sometimes feel overwhelming, especially when dealing with negative content or cyberbullying. Don't hesitate to take a break or limit your usage if it starts impacting your mental well-being.

Staying informed and setting boundaries can make your social media experience safer and more enjoyable.

Key Takeaways

- Social media privacy settings are your first defense against oversharing and unwanted exposure. Regularly review and adjust these to control what others can see.
- Avoid posting personal identifiers, travel plans, and sensitive work information to protect your privacy.
- Use blocking, reporting, and fact-checking tools to avoid harmful content and misinformation, and take breaks if social media becomes overwhelming.

Interactive Activity: Social Media Privacy Checkup

In this activity, let's take a closer look at your own social media accounts and make some privacy adjustments:

1. **Select Two Social Media Accounts**: Pick two accounts (e.g., Facebook, Instagram, Twitter) where you're most active.
2. **Review Privacy Settings**: Log in and go to the privacy settings for each account. Adjust your audience settings for posts, limit profile visibility, and turn off any location-sharing features you don't use.
3. **Audit Your Recent Posts**: Look at your recent posts and see if any might contain information that could be considered oversharing. Decide if you'd like to delete or change the audience for any of them.
4. **Update or Remove Third-Party Access**: Check if any third-party apps are connected to your accounts. Revoke permissions for any apps you don't recognize or no longer need.

NAVIGATING SOCIAL MEDIA SAFELY

Completing this checkup will help you make more informed decisions about what you share online, who can see it, and how to reduce your exposure to risks.

6

Smart Habits for Digital Wellness

In our digital world, it's easy to lose track of time online, experience "information overload," or feel overwhelmed by constant notifications. Digital wellness is about creating a balanced and mindful relationship with technology to protect our mental and emotional health. In this chapter, we'll explore healthy digital habits that help you stay in control of your screen time, manage stress, and foster a positive online experience.

Managing Screen Time

While technology can be incredibly useful, spending too much time on screens can have adverse effects on our physical and mental well-being. Here are a few tips to help you limit and make the most of your screen time:

1. **Set Time Limits on Apps**: Many devices and apps allow you to set time limits. Try setting a daily limit on apps that you find yourself scrolling on for long periods, such as social media or gaming apps.
2. **Create No-Screen Zones**: Establishing areas or times where screens are not allowed, like during family meals or in the bedroom,

can help you unwind and reconnect with people around you.
3. **Use the 20-20-20 Rule**: To reduce eye strain, follow the 20-20-20 rule: every 20 minutes, look at something 20 feet away for 20 seconds. This simple habit helps reduce fatigue and strain from prolonged screen time.
4. **Schedule "Tech-Free" Breaks**: Taking regular breaks from screens throughout the day—like going for a walk or reading a physical book—can refresh your mind and prevent burnout.

Finding a balance in screen time ensures that technology enriches your life rather than consumes it.

Dealing with Digital Stress and Anxiety

Constant notifications, news updates, and comparisons on social media can sometimes lead to stress and anxiety. Here are strategies for managing these pressures:

1. **Limit Notifications**: Customizing your notification settings to only receive the essentials reduces distractions and helps you stay focused on important tasks. Turn off notifications for non-urgent apps to create a calmer online experience.
2. **Set Boundaries on Checking News and Social Media**: Set specific times to check the news or social media instead of continuously scrolling throughout the day. This reduces the tendency to get overwhelmed by a constant stream of information.
3. **Unfollow or Mute Accounts That Cause Negative Feelings**: Your online experience should uplift and inspire you. Don't hesitate to unfollow or mute accounts that cause stress, jealousy, or insecurity.
4. **Practice Digital Mindfulness**: Mindfulness is the practice of staying present in the moment. Applying it to your digital habits

can help you stay aware of when you're using technology for a purpose versus when you're just "zoning out." Before opening an app, pause and ask yourself what you want to accomplish.

By managing digital stress, you make your online life healthier and more positive.

Building a Positive Online Environment

The online communities we join and the content we consume shape our digital experiences. Here are some ways to foster a positive and supportive online environment:

1. **Engage in Positive Interactions**: Aim to share constructive comments, offer support, and celebrate others' achievements. Being positive online not only benefits others but also enhances your own experience.
2. **Curate Uplifting Content**: Follow accounts and join communities that promote learning, personal growth, and positivity. Curating your feed helps ensure that the content you see online adds value to your day.
3. **Practice Good Digital Etiquette**: Treat others with respect, avoid using all-caps (which can come off as yelling), and think carefully before commenting. Good etiquette can help you build better connections and enjoy a more harmonious online experience.
4. **Be Aware of Online Influences**: Recognize that the content you consume affects your thoughts and moods. Reflect on whether the accounts you follow align with your values and contribute to your well-being.

A positive online environment empowers you to use the internet as a tool for connection, learning, and growth.

SMART HABITS FOR DIGITAL WELLNESS

Key Takeaways

- Smart digital habits, like setting screen time limits and practicing the 20-20-20 rule, can help you manage screen time effectively.
- Reducing notifications, setting boundaries, and practicing mindfulness can prevent digital stress and support mental well-being.
- Engaging positively, curating uplifting content, and practicing digital etiquette enhances your online experience and contribute to a supportive community.

Interactive Activity: Personal Digital Wellness Plan

This activity will guide you in creating a personalized plan for digital wellness, based on the principles covered in this chapter. Here's how to get started:

1. **Set a Daily Screen Time Goal**: Decide on a realistic screen time goal that allows you to stay productive while giving you more time away from devices.
2. **Choose One Digital Habit to Focus On**: Select one habit you'd like to improve, such as reducing notifications or limiting social media use.
3. **Identify a "Tech-Free Zone" or Time**: Choose a space or a part of your day that will be tech-free, like the dining room or the first hour after you wake up.
4. **List Three Positive Accounts to Follow**: Think of three accounts that inspire, educate, or support your goals and make a point to engage with them regularly.

By implementing these steps, you'll create a healthier, more balanced relationship with technology that supports both your productivity and your well-being.

7

Recognizing and Avoiding Online Scams

The internet offers convenience and opportunity, but it also creates openings for scammers who seek to deceive and exploit. Scams have become increasingly sophisticated, with attackers using various tactics to trick people into giving away personal information, money, or access to accounts. This chapter will equip you with knowledge on how to recognize, avoid, and respond to common online scams, helping you stay safe in the digital world.

Types of Common Online Scams

Scammers are resourceful, and they adapt to new platforms and trends. Here are some of the most prevalent online scams to watch out for:

1. **Phishing Scams**: Phishing scams involve messages that appear to be from trusted organizations, urging you to click on a link or download an attachment. These links often lead to fake websites designed to steal login credentials or personal data.
2. **Tech Support Scams**: In tech support scams, you might receive a pop-up or call claiming that your computer is infected with

malware, and the "technician" offers to fix it—for a fee. They may try to install harmful software or trick you into giving remote access to your device.

3. **Online Shopping Scams**: Some fake online stores offer items at unbeatable prices to lure shoppers in. Once you make a purchase, the product never arrives, or it's of inferior quality. Scammers may even steal your payment information.

4. **Romance Scams**: In romance scams, someone you meet online builds a relationship with you and eventually asks for money, claiming they have an emergency. These scams exploit trust and emotions to manipulate victims.

5. **Prize or Lottery Scams**: These scams inform you that you've won a large prize or lottery, but to claim it, you need to pay a "processing fee" or provide personal information. Genuine lotteries and prizes never require payments to claim a reward.

By being aware of these scams and their tactics, you can spot warning signs before falling victim.

How to Identify a Potential Scam

Spotting scams often comes down to looking for red flags. Here are some common signs that a message, offer, or request might be a scam:

1. **Urgent or Threatening Language**: Scams often use urgency to pressure victims. Phrases like "Act now or lose access!" or "This is your last chance!" are designed to make you panic and act without thinking.

2. **Requests for Personal Information**: Be wary of any unsolicited message asking for sensitive information, such as Social Security numbers, passwords, or payment details. Legitimate companies rarely request this type of information via email or text.

RECOGNIZING AND AVOIDING ONLINE SCAMS

3. **Too-Good-to-Be-True Offers**: If an offer seems incredibly generous, such as an unbelievable discount or "free money," it's likely a scam. Scammers use enticing offers to capture your attention and gain access to your personal data.
4. **Unfamiliar Email Addresses or Links**: Many phishing emails come from email addresses that look similar to official ones but contain small differences. Always double-check the sender's email, and if something feels off, go to the company's official website rather than clicking links.
5. **Requests for Payments via Gift Cards or Wire Transfers**: Scammers often ask for payments in forms that are difficult to trace, like gift cards, cryptocurrency, or wire transfers. Legitimate businesses rarely request these payment methods.

By staying vigilant and recognizing these warning signs, you can reduce your chances of falling victim to scams.

Steps to Avoid Online Scams

Taking preventative actions is key to staying safe online. Here are some effective steps to avoid falling for scams:

1. **Verify Before You Trust**: If you receive an unexpected message or call, verify its authenticity. For example, if a message claims to be from your bank, call the bank's official number to confirm.
2. **Avoid Clicking Unknown Links or Attachments**: Scammers often use links or attachments to trick you into downloading malware or visiting fake sites. Avoid clicking on anything from unfamiliar senders, and always hover over links to check where they lead.
3. **Use Strong and Unique Passwords**: Strong passwords help protect your accounts in case scammers try to breach them. Use

unique passwords for each account to reduce the impact if one account is compromised.
4. **Enable Two-Factor Authentication (2FA)**: 2FA adds an extra layer of security to your accounts by requiring a second form of verification, such as a code sent to your phone. This makes it harder for scammers to access your accounts even if they have your password.
5. **Monitor Your Accounts Regularly**: Regularly check your bank and credit card statements for unusual activity. Promptly report any suspicious transactions to your bank to reduce the risk of financial loss.

These steps can help keep your information and finances safe from scammers.

Key Takeaways

- Online scams come in many forms, including phishing, tech support scams, and fake shopping sites. Being aware of these types can help you identify scams before falling for them.
- Scammers often use urgency, too-good-to-be-true offers, and requests for sensitive information as red flags. Recognizing these tactics is critical to staying safe.
- Practical measures like verifying messages, avoiding unknown links, and using two-factor authentication can protect you from scams.

Interactive Activity: Scam Spotting Exercise

This exercise will help you practice identifying potential scams by examining common scam tactics. Follow these steps:

RECOGNIZING AND AVOIDING ONLINE SCAMS

1. **Review a List of Sample Messages**: Look at a sample of emails or text messages (which you could print or find online) that mimic common scam attempts, such as phishing or fake tech support emails.
2. **Identify Red Flags**: For each message, circle or highlight red flags, such as urgent language, unfamiliar email addresses, or requests for personal information.
3. **Practice Verification**: For each sample, think about what you would do to verify the legitimacy of the message. For example, would you call a company's official number or check for information on their website?
4. **Discuss with a Friend or Family Member**: If possible, go through this activity with someone else and discuss your observations. Comparing thoughts can help sharpen your scam-spotting skills.

By practicing with real examples, you'll be better equipped to recognize scams in your own online interactions.

8

Protecting Your Digital Identity

In today's online world, our digital identities are a mix of personal information, financial details, and online behaviors that, together, form a valuable profile. Protecting your digital identity is essential to prevent unauthorized access, identity theft, and privacy invasions. This chapter explores steps you can take to safeguard your digital identity, manage your digital footprint, and maintain control over your personal information.

Understanding Your Digital Footprint

Your digital footprint is the trail of data you leave behind whenever you use the internet. This includes everything from social media posts to search history and even metadata from photos. There are two types of digital footprints:

1. **Active Footprint**: This is data you intentionally share, like posts on social media, comments on blogs, or reviews on websites.
2. **Passive Footprint**: This data is collected without your direct input, such as your browsing habits, location data, or device information.

PROTECTING YOUR DIGITAL IDENTITY

While our digital footprints make it easier to personalize online experiences, they also make us more visible to potential hackers and companies collecting data for targeted advertising.

Controlling Your Digital Footprint

Being mindful of your digital footprint helps you control what information about you is available online. Here are some steps to manage it effectively:

1. **Search for Yourself Online**: Start by typing your name into a search engine to see what information is publicly available. This allows you to address anything you'd prefer to keep private.
2. **Limit Personal Information on Social Media**: Avoid oversharing, especially details like your full birthdate, address, or work location. Adjust privacy settings to control who can view your posts and profile.
3. **Be Cautious with Location Sharing**: Many apps track and share location data by default. Check location settings on your phone and adjust app permissions to control when and how location information is shared.
4. **Request Deletion of Old or Unused Accounts**: Dormant accounts can be vulnerable to breaches. Take time to delete any old social media, shopping, or email accounts you no longer use.
5. **Review Permissions Regularly**: Frequently review permissions for apps on your phone and revoke any that seem unnecessary or invasive. Be particularly cautious with apps that request access to your contacts, camera, and location.

Taking these steps reduces your online visibility and helps keep your personal information private.

Creating Strong Passwords and Protecting Account Access

A strong password is a crucial defense against unauthorized access. Here's how to create and manage secure passwords:

1. **Use a Combination of Characters**: A strong password includes upper- and lowercase letters, numbers, and symbols. Avoid using personal information like birthdays or pet names.
2. **Create Unique Passwords for Each Account**: Using the same password across multiple accounts makes it easier for hackers to gain access. Create different passwords for each account, especially for sensitive sites like email or banking.
3. **Consider a Password Manager**: A password manager securely stores your passwords and can generate complex, unique passwords for each account. This simplifies password management and increases security.
4. **Enable Two-Factor Authentication (2FA)**: 2FA provides an extra layer of security by requiring a second form of verification (like a text code) to access your accounts. Enable 2FA on any account that offers it, particularly for financial, email, and social media accounts.
5. **Change Passwords Regularly**: Routine password changes reduce the risk of unauthorized access in case of data breaches. Aim to update your passwords every few months.

These practices create a strong line of defense to keep your accounts and information secure.

Recognizing Identity Theft and What to Do

Identity theft occurs when someone steals your personal information to impersonate you or commit fraud. Recognizing the warning signs early can help you address the situation before it escalates.

PROTECTING YOUR DIGITAL IDENTITY

1. **Unusual Activity on Bank Accounts**: Watch for unfamiliar transactions on your bank and credit card statements. Small charges from unknown vendors could signal fraud.
2. **Unexpected Changes in Credit Score**: Sudden changes in your credit score could mean that new accounts have been opened in your name. Regularly monitor your credit report for unexpected changes.
3. **Unrecognized Accounts or Loans**: If you're notified of an account or loan you didn't open, it's essential to act immediately. Contact the company and report the fraudulent activity.
4. **Receiving Mail for Accounts You Didn't Open**: Receiving unexpected bills or notifications for accounts or services you didn't sign up for could indicate that your information has been used by someone else.
5. **Missing Mail or Bills**: If your regular mail or bills stop arriving, it's possible that someone has redirected your mail to gain access to your information.

If you suspect identity theft, contact your bank, report it to the Federal Trade Commission (FTC), and consider freezing your credit to prevent new accounts from being opened in your name.

Key Takeaways

- Your digital footprint consists of all data left behind during online interactions. Actively managing your footprint limits your visibility and protects your privacy.
- Strong passwords, unique for each account, and two-factor authentication are essential tools to secure your accounts.
- Recognizing warning signs of identity theft, like unauthorized transactions or unexpected credit changes, enables you to act

quickly to protect your financial health.

Interactive Activity: Digital Identity Checkup

In this activity, you'll take steps to strengthen your digital identity protection with a brief checkup:

1. **Run a Search of Your Name**: Conduct an internet search using your full name, and note any websites or information that reveal personal details. Request deletion where possible.
2. **Create a Unique Password**: Pick one account and change the password to something complex and unique. Try using a password manager to help generate and store this password.
3. **Enable Two-Factor Authentication (2FA)**: Choose one of your high-risk accounts, like email or banking, and enable 2FA if you haven't already.
4. **Review Social Media Privacy Settings**: Go through your privacy settings on social media and adjust them to limit what others can see.

This checkup helps establish good habits to keep your digital identity safe and private.

9

Building a Responsible and Positive Digital Reputation

As we navigate the digital world, every post, comment, and interaction contributes to our digital reputation. Just like a reputation in the real world, a digital reputation reflects how others perceive us based on our online actions and behaviors. This chapter explores the importance of building a positive and responsible digital presence, how to manage it effectively, and the long-term benefits it brings to both personal and professional lives.

Why Your Digital Reputation Matters

Your digital reputation can affect various aspects of your life. Whether applying for college, a job, or joining new communities, others may look at your online presence to form an impression of who you are. Here are a few reasons why your digital reputation is essential:

1. **Employability and Career Opportunities**: Many employers check social media profiles and online presence before hiring. A positive reputation can increase your chances, while a negative one could be a setback.

2. **Academic and Community Involvement**: Schools and volunteer organizations often review digital reputations to gauge candidates' behavior and character. Building a respectful and engaging presence can open doors to new opportunities.
3. **Trust and Relationships**: A strong digital reputation can help you build meaningful connections and friendships. Conversely, a history of negative behavior can harm relationships and reduce trust.

Understanding the impact of your digital actions encourages you to be mindful and intentional with how you interact online.

Building a Positive Digital Reputation

Creating a responsible and positive digital presence doesn't require you to avoid online interactions but rather to approach them thoughtfully. Here are ways to ensure that your online actions reflect well on you:

1. **Be Respectful in All Interactions**: Practice kindness, empathy, and respect in comments and messages, even during disagreements. Avoid name-calling, derogatory language, and spreading negativity.
2. **Share Constructive and Positive Content**: Contribute content that adds value, such as sharing educational resources, celebrating achievements, or promoting important causes. This helps you become a positive influence in your online communities.
3. **Stay Informed and Aware**: Stay updated on digital etiquette, privacy practices, and security recommendations. This shows responsibility and awareness, which strengthens your reputation.
4. **Credit Others' Work**: If you share others' posts, artwork, or ideas, make sure to credit them appropriately. Giving credit shows

BUILDING A RESPONSIBLE AND POSITIVE DIGITAL REPUTATION

integrity and respect for others' contributions.
5. **Be Honest and Transparent**: Authenticity is key to a positive reputation. Avoid embellishing details or sharing false information about yourself, as honesty fosters trust with others.

By approaching online interactions with integrity, you build a digital reputation that reflects your values and principles.

Managing Mistakes and Moving Forward

Nobody is perfect, and occasionally, mistakes happen. If you've made a comment you regret or shared something inaccurate, here's how to handle it:

1. **Delete or Edit Content**: For minor issues, consider deleting or editing the post to correct the mistake. Make a habit of reviewing your old posts and cleaning up anything that no longer aligns with the image you want to present.
2. **Apologize if Necessary**: If you hurt someone or made a harmful comment, a sincere apology can help repair the situation. Taking accountability shows maturity and responsibility.
3. **Learn and Grow**: Mistakes can be learning experiences. Reflect on what you can do differently in the future to ensure that your digital interactions align with your goals and values.
4. **Move On with Positive Actions**: Focus on consistently positive online behaviors. Over time, a pattern of positive actions can outweigh the occasional misstep.

Handling mistakes professionally and sincerely shows that you're willing to grow, which can strengthen your reputation in the long run.

Creating a Personal Brand

A "personal brand" is the image and reputation you want others to associate with you online. Building a personal brand is especially useful for professionals and students looking to showcase their skills, interests, and values. Here's how to start:

1. **Define Your Online Goals**: Think about what you want others to know about you. Is it your creativity, technical skills, or leadership qualities? Knowing this helps you shape a consistent and intentional online presence.
2. **Choose Your Platforms Wisely**: Not all platforms are suited for professional branding. LinkedIn is ideal for professional networking, while Instagram and Twitter can showcase creativity or interests. Focus on the platforms that align with your goals.
3. **Be Consistent**: Consistency across platforms strengthens your personal brand. Use similar profile pictures, maintain a professional tone, and stick to topics that reflect your goals.
4. **Engage in Relevant Communities**: Follow and engage with groups, accounts, or forums that reflect your interests. Active engagement in these spaces shows that you're involved and committed to learning.

Building a personal brand that reflects your interests, values, and skills can open doors to professional and personal growth.

Key Takeaways

- Your digital reputation can impact your future opportunities and relationships. Maintaining a positive presence reflects well on your character.
- Being respectful, authentic, and thoughtful online helps you build a positive digital reputation that reflects your values.

BUILDING A RESPONSIBLE AND POSITIVE DIGITAL REPUTATION

- Handling mistakes responsibly and building a personal brand strengthens your online presence and contributes to long-term success.

Interactive Activity: Your Digital Reputation Assessment

This final activity allows you to assess your current digital reputation and develop a plan for any adjustments you'd like to make:

1. **Review Your Online Presence**: Visit your social media profiles and Google yourself. Note any content that doesn't align with the digital reputation you want to build.
2. **Identify Three Positive Actions**: Write down three actions you can take to enhance your reputation, like updating your profile information, engaging with positive content, or removing old posts.
3. **Define Your Personal Brand Statement**: Write a brief sentence or two summarizing what you want your online reputation to represent (e.g., "I aim to be a positive, thoughtful voice in online tech communities.")
4. **Create a Plan for Improvement**: Make a list of small, realistic steps you can take over the next few weeks to align your online presence with your brand statement.

This assessment helps you develop a mindful and intentional approach to building a positive digital reputation that aligns with your goals.

10

Bringing It All Together: Your Path to a Safer Digital Life

Throughout this book, we've explored what it means to stay safe and make responsible choices in our digital lives. By learning about the key areas of online privacy, digital etiquette, cybersecurity, and personal reputation, you now have a solid toolkit to help you navigate the online world with confidence and awareness.

In this final chapter, we'll summarize the journey we've taken together, revisit the most important takeaways, and discuss how you can continue building these digital skills for a safe and positive online experience.

Your Digital Safety Journey: Key Takeaways

Here's a quick recap of the essential points we've covered:

1. **Understanding Digital Safety and Awareness**: You've learned why digital safety is essential and how even small actions online can have a big impact on privacy, security, and reputation.
2. **Protecting Your Privacy**: Privacy settings, limiting personal data exposure, and being mindful about sharing are simple steps that keep your personal information safe from potential misuse.

BRINGING IT ALL TOGETHER: YOUR PATH TO A SAFER DIGITAL LIFE

3. **Recognizing and Avoiding Online Threats**: Whether it's phishing, malware, or social engineering, being able to identify common threats is your first line of defense against cyberattacks.
4. **Using Social Media Responsibly**: Social media is a powerful tool for connection and self-expression, but it also requires careful handling. Practicing good privacy habits and staying alert to social media scams keeps your experience positive.
5. **Safe Online Shopping and Banking**: When it comes to sharing sensitive financial information, understanding what makes a website secure helps you shop and bank with confidence.
6. **Preventing Cyberbullying and Promoting Kindness Online**: Online interactions have real-life impacts. By being a positive force and knowing how to respond to cyberbullying, you help create a kinder digital space.
7. **Securing Your Devices**: Regular updates, antivirus software, and strong passwords protect your devices and data from malware and unauthorized access.
8. **Safeguarding Your Digital Identity**: By managing your digital footprint and using secure, unique passwords, you protect your online identity and reduce the risk of identity theft.
9. **Building a Responsible Digital Reputation**: Your online reputation matters. Maintaining a positive digital presence and handling mistakes thoughtfully helps you create a reputation you're proud of.

Applying These Skills in Everyday Life

These digital safety skills are not just for reading—they're for practicing every day. As you engage online, apply the principles from each chapter to help you navigate with a mindful, safety-first approach:

- **Think Before You Share**: Make it a habit to consider privacy and long-term effects before sharing anything online.
- **Stay Informed**: The digital world is constantly changing, so stay up-to-date on new security measures, emerging threats, and digital trends.
- **Teach and Share**: Digital safety is for everyone, and you can help others by sharing what you've learned with family, friends, and even coworkers. The more people know, the safer online spaces become for everyone.

The Road Ahead: Growing as a Digital Citizen

As you continue your digital journey, remember that being a responsible digital citizen is an ongoing process. This book is just the beginning, and each interaction, each platform, and each piece of content you engage with provides an opportunity to grow as a thoughtful and proactive digital user.

Building a positive digital legacy—one based on safety, respect, and integrity—has a lasting impact not only on you but also on the broader online community. Every time you choose to protect your privacy, engage respectfully, and promote kindness, you contribute to a healthier, safer digital world.

Closing Thoughts

The internet offers incredible opportunities for learning, connecting, and growing. By practicing the digital safety habits and values in this book, you can enjoy those opportunities with peace of mind. Remember, digital safety isn't about avoiding the online world; it's about empowering yourself to explore it wisely and responsibly.

With the skills you've gained, you're now ready to click smart, stay safe, and make the most of your online experiences. Thank you for

BRINGING IT ALL TOGETHER: YOUR PATH TO A SAFER DIGITAL LIFE

taking this journey toward a safer digital life.

Key Takeaways

- Digital safety is a journey, and each skill contributes to a safer, more positive online experience.
- Applying what you've learned—privacy habits, device security, responsible interactions—will help you navigate the internet confidently.
- Being a responsible digital citizen means sharing this knowledge and setting a positive example for others.

Interactive Activity: Your Digital Safety Commitment

As a final step, take a few moments to write your personal digital safety commitment. This could include specific actions you plan to maintain, like checking privacy settings monthly, creating unique passwords for each account, or practicing online kindness.

Your commitment could look something like this:

"I commit to protecting my digital safety by practicing mindful sharing, maintaining strong security habits, and contributing to positive online spaces. I will stay informed, stay respectful, and always prioritize safety in my digital interactions."

This commitment can serve as a reminder to you and inspire others to follow safe digital practices.

Enjoyed This Book? We'd Love to Hear From You!

Thank you for joining us on this journey to a safer, smarter digital life! If Click Smart, Stay Safe helped you gain valuable insights or encouraged you to take a fresh look at your digital habits, please consider leaving a review.

Your feedback helps us reach more readers who want to build their digital safety skills and can guide us as we create more resources to help people navigate today's online world. Every review makes a difference, and we'd love to hear your thoughts—whether it's what you enjoyed most or how this book impacted your approach to digital safety.

Thank you for helping us create a safer, more informed digital community. Click smart, stay safe, and keep spreading the word!

Glossary

- **2FA (Two-Factor Authentication)**: An extra layer of security requiring two forms of verification to access an account, such as a password and a one-time code sent to your phone.
- **Adware**: Software that displays unwanted advertisements on your device, often as pop-ups, and sometimes collects your data for targeted ads.
- **Antivirus Software**: A program designed to detect and remove viruses, malware, and other harmful software from your devices.
- **Botnet**: A network of infected devices controlled remotely by hackers to perform large-scale attacks or spam activities without the device owner's knowledge.
- **Cyberbullying**: Bullying that takes place over digital devices or platforms, such as sending hurtful messages, spreading rumors, or embarrassing someone online.
- **Data Breach**: An incident in which personal or confidential information is accessed without permission, often resulting in exposure or theft of sensitive data.
- **Digital Footprint**: The trail of data you leave online through activities like browsing, social media posts, and shopping. Your digital footprint can be active (intentional) or passive (collected without your direct input).
- **Encryption**: The process of converting information into a code to prevent unauthorized access, used to protect data during transmis-

sion or storage.

- **Firewall**: A security system that monitors and controls incoming and outgoing network traffic to prevent unauthorized access to your device or network.
- **Hacker**: A person who uses their computer skills to access systems, networks, or data without permission. Not all hackers are malicious—some are "ethical hackers" who help improve security.
- **Identity Theft**: The act of stealing someone's personal information to impersonate them or commit fraud, often leading to financial and reputational damage for the victim.
- **IP Address**: A unique string of numbers assigned to each device connected to the internet, identifying the device's location within a network.
- **Malware**: Malicious software designed to harm or exploit any programmable device, network, or service. Types include viruses, worms, trojans, and ransomware.
- **Password Manager**: A tool that stores and organizes your passwords securely, helping you create complex, unique passwords without having to remember each one.
- **Personal Brand**: The unique image or reputation you create and present online, often reflecting your values, skills, and interests.
- **Phishing**: A type of scam in which a person is tricked into giving away sensitive information (like passwords or credit card details) by posing as a trustworthy entity, often via email.
- **Ransomware**: A type of malware that locks your device or encrypts your files until a ransom is paid to unlock access.
- **Social Engineering**: Manipulative tactics used to trick people into revealing confidential information or performing actions that compromise security.
- **Spam**: Unwanted messages or emails, often used to promote products, phishing scams, or spread malware. Spam can clog

inboxes and waste time.
- **Spyware**: Malicious software that secretly monitors your activity and collects information, often used to gather personal details without your knowledge.
- **Two-Step Verification**: Similar to two-factor authentication, it adds a second step to verify your identity, like a text code or fingerprint, after entering your password.
- **VPN (Virtual Private Network)**: A tool that masks your IP address and encrypts your internet connection, providing extra privacy and security when browsing.
- **Virus**: A type of malware that replicates itself and spreads to other devices, often causing harm to files, programs, or the entire system.
- **Web Browser**: A software application (like Chrome, Firefox, or Safari) used to access websites and navigate the internet.
- **Wi-Fi Security**: Measures to protect wireless networks, often using encryption methods (like WPA2) to prevent unauthorized access to your network.

Citation

1. **Federal Trade Commission.** (n.d.). *Protecting Your Privacy Online.* FTC Consumer Information. Retrieved from https://www.consumer.ftc.gov/topics/privacy-identity-online-security
2. **National Cybersecurity Alliance.** (2023). *Stay Safe Online: Security Tips and Tools for Families and Businesses.* Retrieved from https://staysafeonline.org/
3. **Cyberbullying Research Center.** (2023). *What is Cyberbullying? Facts and Information.* Retrieved from https://cyberbullying.org/
4. **Microsoft Digital Safety.** (2023). *Digital Safety Tools and Tips.* Microsoft Corporation. Retrieved from https://www.microsoft.com/en-us/safety
5. **Internet Society.** (2023). *A Parent's Guide to Online Privacy and Security.* Internet Society. Retrieved from https://www.internetsociety.org/
6. **Symantec.** (2023). *Internet Security Threat Report.* Symantec Corporation. Retrieved from https://www.broadcom.com/company/newsroom/press-releases
7. **National Institute of Standards and Technology (NIST).** (2023). *Framework for Improving Critical Infrastructure Cybersecurity.* NIST. Retrieved from https://www.nist.gov/cyberframework
8. **Electronic Frontier Foundation (EFF).** (2023). *Protecting Your Digital Privacy.* Retrieved from https://www.eff.org/issues/privacy

CITATION

9. **Common Sense Media**. (2023). *Digital Literacy and Online Safety for Kids*. Common Sense Media. Retrieved from https://www.commonsensemedia.org/
10. **Google Safety Center**. (n.d.). *Tips for Staying Safe Online*. Google LLC. Retrieved from https://safety.google/
11. **Center for Cyber Safety and Education**. (2023). *Cyber Safety Tips and Resources for Families*. Retrieved from https://iamcybersafe.org/

Disclaimer

This book includes general advice and best practices related to digital safety, cybersecurity, and online etiquette. While every effort has been made to ensure the accuracy of this information, readers are encouraged to consult official resources or experts for specific guidance, particularly as technology and online threats evolve.

www.ingramcontent.com/pod-product-compliance
Lightning Source LLC
Chambersburg PA
CBHW070427240526
45472CB00020B/1493